# BESIEGING THE CASTLE OF LADIES

**Library of Congress Cataloging-in-Publication Data**

Greene, Thomas M.
Besieging the castle of ladies / Thomas M. Greene.
p. cm.– (Occasional papers / Center for Medieval & Early Renaissance Studies ; no. 4)
Includes bibliographical references (p.).
ISBN 0–86698–145–4
1. Arthurian romances—History and criticism. 2. Knights and knighthood in literature. I. Title. II. Series: Occasional papers (State University of New York at Binghamton. Medieval & Renaissance Texts & Studies): no. 4.
PN685.G74 1994
809'.93353–dc20 94–40662
CIP

This book is made to last.
It is set in Bembo, smythe-sewn
and printed on acid-free paper
to library specifications.

Printed in the United States of America

THOMAS M. GREENE

# BESIEGING THE CASTLE OF LADIES

OCCASIONAL PAPERS, NO. 4

CENTER FOR MEDIEVAL & EARLY RENAISSANCE STUDIES

MEDIEVAL & RENAISSANCE TEXTS & STUDIES
Binghamton, New York
1995

# *List of Illustrations*

Fig. 1. Reproduced from Roger Sherman Loomis, "The Allegorical Siege in the Art of the Middle Ages," *American Journal of Archaeology*, 2nd s., 23 (1919): 260. 9

Figs. 2a and b. Reproduced from Walter de Milemete, *De nobilitatibus, sapientiis, et prudentiis regum.*(Facsimile edition with introduction by M. R. James. The Roxburghe Club, 1913.) 12

Fig. 3. Reproduced from Raymond Koechlin, *Les Ivoires gothiques français* (Paris: Picard, 1924), vol. 2, #1282. 14

Fig. 4. Reproduced from O. Beigbeder, "Le Chateau d'amour dans l'ivoirerie et son symbolisme," *Gazette des Beaux-Arts* 38 (1951): 74. 16

Fig. 5. Reproduced from Jules Guiffrey, *Histoire générale de la tapisserie* (no place or date indicated; apparently early twentieth century), vol. 3. 28

for Walter Cahn

# *Besieging the Castle of Ladies*

THE SUBJECT OF THIS PAPER is a protean iconographical motif, a certain kind of symbolic castle, which turns up in various cultural contexts throughout western Europe across several centuries. We meet it first in central European legend; later it surfaces in medieval folklore, later in poetry and the visual arts, and still later in courtly festivities of the Renaissance. Variants can be traced in Renaissance romance and drama. It is in fact by no means easy to delimit the widening circles of its versions and variations. Nor is it always easy to interpret the meaning of its symbolism (if indeed interpretation is called for), any more than it is easy to say where the iconographic tradition began. To follow the progress of this topos is to confront interpretive puzzles in a narrative riddled with gaps. Nonetheless there *is* a narrative, which I want to begin *in medias res* with a single memorable instance which will anchor us in time and space and to which we can return for intermittent enlightenment.

The date is Friday, November 19th, 1501. The occasion is a royal banquet in Westminster Hall, where the court of king Henry VII of England is celebrating the wedding, already performed, of the frail adolescent prince Arthur Tudor, heir apparent to the English throne, to the adolescent princess Catherine of Aragon. Present at this entertainment are the king and queen, the young bride and bridegroom, a company of English notables and the princess's Spanish entourage. Also present with the others is the groom's ten-year-old brother, the duke of York, future King Henry VIII and future husband to Catherine. What concerns us is the entertainment, or disguising as it was called, performed to divert the royal guests on this particular evening. We are fortunate to possess a highly detailed account of it by an anonymous eye-witness.[1]

This disguising, produced by the gifted Tudor impresario William Cornish, made use for the first time in England of a device familiar in Burgundian court festivity, the pageant car, which was a large wheeled platform supporting a fanciful or allegorical structure. On this Friday evening, the first pageant car which was drawn into the banqueting hall bore a castle, large enough to contain eight young women visible through its windows, as well as four boys dressed as maidens singing sweetly, according to our report, in the castle's four turrets. The second car bore a ship, realistically fitted with rigging and mariners as well as a young woman dressed to resemble the princess Catherine. After the ship had taken its place, two envoys named Hope and Desire disembarked and made their way to the castle, where they introduced themselves to the eight ladies as envoys of the Knights of the Mount of Love, who were suitors for the ladies'

---

[1] My paraphrases and quotations of this report are taken from *The Receyt of the Ladie Kateryne*, ed. Gordon Kipling (Oxford: Early English Text Society, Oxford University Press, 1990), 55–58. For a discussion of the disguising, see Kipling's *The Triumph of Honor* (Leiden: Leiden University Press, 1977), 102–5.

favors, as they put it, "of the mattir of love." When the ladies brusquely refused, the ambassadors Hope and Desire warned that this conduct was likely to offend the Knights of the Mount of Love and might lead to serious consequences. And indeed, the third and last pageant car now made an appearance bearing the Mount of Love with its eight knights, who, when informed by their envoys of the ladies' disdainful behavior, did assault the castle successfully and forced the ladies to surrender. After this victory, the knights led the ladies out to dance, whereupon it appeared that half the dancers of each gender were wearing English costume and the other half Spanish. With that celebration of international and sexual harmony, the disguising came to an end.

This entertainment makes many claims on our interest, more than we can pursue here. In the perspective of the history of English court festivity, it marks an important date. It brought together spectacle, symbolism, narrative, and dance in an organic unity which was new and which anticipated the splendors and follies of the Stuart masque. One specialist has described it as "the most significant of all early Tudor court entertainments."[2] But for us, it also offers an opportunity to consider that motif which will concern us in this paper, the siege by men of a castle defended by women. It can be assumed that this device was well received, since it would be repeated twice at court during the succeeding reign: first, in 1512, a *Fortresse dangerus* containing six ladies was successfully captured by assailants, including King Henry; and again in 1522 a "schatew vert," another castle of ladies—one of them a certain Anne Boleyn—was stormed by eight lords, again led by the king. In each case the assault was followed by a dance.

There is much in that first disguising that deserves discussion, but before considering it, I want to make a long historical di-

[2] Sydney Anglo, "William Cornish in a Play, Pageants, Prison, and Politics," *Review of English Studies* n.s. 10 (1959): 353.

gression, since Cornish's device had a complex pre-history which may help us to understand it. What evidence we have suggests that it emerged from untraceable roots in the imagination of the Dark Ages. The earliest castle of women known to me appears as a foundation myth of the city of Prague in the chronicle of a certain Cosmas of Prague, composed early in the twelfth century. Cosmas relates that a Bohemian queen named Lubossa surrounded herself with a group of Amazons who bore arms, dressed like men, hunted game, and received the male visitors they chose, when they chose. So independent were they that they constructed a fortress for themselves on a suitable site, a fortress which was named "Devin," meaning "Castle of Maidens." This led the young men of the region to build their own castle nearby, with the result that a state of intermittent warfare prevailed between the two genders. This came to an end only when both sides agreed on a truce of three days and a festive communal banquet; the truce effectively concluded the women's period of freedom, since during the evening of the first day, each youth seized a maiden and made off with her. The next morning Devin was burned and a peace treaty signed. After that violence and after the death of Queen Lubossa, writes Cosmas, the wives of our country have always remained subject to the power of their husbands. Under these auspices, recalling the analogous legend of the Sabine women, the city of Prague witnessed its foundation.[3] This narrative, which locates the beginnings of community in male mastery, does not describe a formal siege or a drawn battle between the genders, but its evocation of a fortress defended by women does furnish the kernel of an image which would have a long future. The legend already invests the castle motif with a theme which will cling to it—the struggle for erotic control.

[3] For the text of Cosmas's account, see the appendix.

This is a harsh foundation myth and a harsh beginning to my narrative. When we cross the line separating legend from history, we do not escape further discord, although in this instance it is not ostensibly between genders. I speak of history because fragmentary evidence indicates that mock-sieges of castles of women were staged in real life on festive occasions at least as early as the thirteenth century. The earliest known performance of such a siege occurred in the town of Treviso in the year 1214. We only know of this occurrence because it ended in disaster; there may have been any number of precedents which went unrecorded. According to the thirteenth-century chronicler Rolandino of Padua, the Podestà of his city decreed that a holiday be celebrated by the construction of a castle, to be graced by twelve of the noblest, most beautiful, and most mirth-loving ladies of the community.[4] These ladies, assisted by their serving-women, defended their fortress against its male assailants; the missiles used by both parties included fruit, nuts, flowers, and spices. Trouble broke out when a group of young bucks from Venice appeared to dispute the gateway with the Paduans; the violence which ensued produced a written record and thus ensured our own knowledge of the event. This *ludus*, as Rolandino calls it, may have been unique, but it was more likely a familiar type of festivity. There are reports at any rate of similar celebrations in the Swiss town of Fribourg lasting for several centuries. The reports evoke wooden castles containing ladies besieged by men, roses used for missiles, the surrender of the castle, a pairing off of defenders and attackers, followed by a procession through the town.[5] Why was this done? One hypothesis would

[4] *Rolandini Patavini de factis in Marchia Tarvisina libri II*, in Lodovico Antonio Muratori, ed., *Rerum italicarum scriptores*, vol. 8 (Milan, 1726), 180–81. English translation in *A Medieval Garner*, ed. G. G. Coulton (London: Constable, 1910), 268–70.

[5] Anon., "Le Siège du chateau d'amour," *Mémoires . . . de la Société Royale des Antiquaires de France*, (1817), 1:186–87.

be that a kind of magic underlies this festivity, magic intended to maintain symbolic control over the potentially contentious realm of gender relations. If the possible frowardness or resistance of women could be overcome in a public show of reconciliation, then the performative symbols might be efficacious in maintaining communal order.

We don't know how many other communities adopted similar mating rituals which have disappeared from view, but doubtless we can safely conjecture that the ones we know were not unique. What could not have been predicted is that the siege by knights of a castle of ladies would become a popular subject in the decorative arts of the later Middle Ages. One does find examples, however, some extant and some lost but recorded in inventories, of illuminated manuscripts, of silverwork, of tapestries, of enamels, and most abundantly of ivories illustrating this subject.[6] Art historians have not succeeded in locating a textual source for these images, and have been forced to hypothesize a lost chivalric romance. Hermeneutically, the abundance of these objects doesn't facilitate generalizations; one can read into them male fantasies of conquest but also male fears of female aggression, expressions of hostility but also of tenderness. Female fantasies, as we shall see, are apparently represented as well.

Of this large body of visual material, the first extant image, to my knowledge, appeared toward the beginning of the fourteenth century as an illumination to the English Peterborough Psalter now in Brussels (Fig. 1), and like many of the surviving illuminations it is not calculated to sweeten relations between genders.

---

[6] The fullest treatment of the visual materials I have found is contained in an old article by Roger Sherman Loomis, "The Allegorical Siege in the Art of the Middle Ages," *American Journal of Archaeology*, 2nd s., 23 (1919): 255–69. Although on a few minor points this article seems to me misleading, I am generally indebted to it.

Fig. 1. *Siege of the Castle of Love.* Peterborough Psalter. Early fourteenth century. Bibliothèque royale, Brussels.

Here four knights armed with swords and wearing chain armor fail to capture a crenellated fortress whose female defenders have much the best of the conflict. At the ground level, two women armed only with roses defend the open gateway against two knights who are about to drop their swords. Above, on a lower platform, four women repel the other pair of knights with roses and crossbow. In the middle of a higher platform sits a crowned queen, flanked by two women holding banners and, at both corners, two more defenders hurling their flowery missiles. There seems little fear that the occupants will hold their fort.[7]

In a double illumination from another English manuscript circa 1326 now at Christ Church College, Oxford (Figs. 2a and b), the four determined female defenders armed with bows and roses do not even allow the males to approach; the knights who are mounted but unarmed can only wring their hands or spread their arms in dismay when confronted by that resolute resistance. In this image, women do certainly appear to be in control. And yet of course the women's weapons are only roses; even the arrows are adorned with roses as though to blunt their force, if indeed there are arrows at all. It isn't easy today to measure the dosage of self-mockery, misogyny, playfulness, fear, and farce that inspired images like these, which have nothing to do with the texts they decorate. The modern student can only recognize that the comedy here, like most interesting comedy, has its roots in deep and shifting layers of feeling.[8]

---

[7] On the Peterborough manuscript, see Lucy Freeman Sandler, *Gothic Manuscripts, 1285–1385* (London and New York, 1986), 45–47, as well as her monograph *The Peterborough Psalter in Brussels and Other Fenland Manuscripts* (London, 1974). See also L. Carolus-Barré, "Le Psautier de Peterborough et ses miniatures profanes," *Romania* 71 (1950): 79–98, especially 88–90. I owe these references to my colleague Walter Cahn.

[8] Walter de Milemete, *De nobilitatibus, sapientiis, et prudentiis regum*, intro. M. R. James. Facsimile ed. (London: The Roxburghe Club, 1913).

Most of our extant visual images of the castle of ladies are not found in manuscripts but rather on ivory caskets and mirror cases produced chiefly in Paris during the fourteenth century.[9] This means that they were not produced primarily for a male audience, as manuscripts were, but for the dressing tables of wealthy aristocratic women. Among that audience, they were clearly very popular. Many of these ivories picture a joust between two mounted knights in the lower center, sometimes announced by heralds with horns, but for our purposes the important action takes place on the side panels and above. On a representative casket in the Victoria and Albert Museum (Fig. 3), we can make out a siege machine on the lower right, a ballista which two footsoldiers are filling with roses, while above them a knight is helping himself to their supply in order to launch his own. On the lower left, a mounted archer is at work with his bow and arrow; a fellow soldier is climbing a siege ladder; still another has climbed a tree to better his position. Between the towers left and right women are hurling their own roses down on the attackers, aided by the god of love himself with bow and arrow. What is surprising however is to find three pairs of lovers on the battlements who are anything but hostile. One of the knights on the left even seems to be on his knees in front of his mistress. It appears that to scale the fortress walls is to win the heart of the lady; the metaphor is acted out in the contrast between the outer panels, where the struggle is still going on, and the inner ones, where it has reached an apparently harmonious conclusion. The relevance of the jousting in the center is unclear, but there may

[9] The standard study of medieval ivories remains Raymond Koechlin, *Les Ivoires gothiques français*, 3 vols. (Paris: Picard, 1924). The article by O. Beigbeder, "Le Chateau d'amour dans l'ivoirerie et son symbolisme," *Gazette des Beaux-Arts* 38 (1951): 65–76, contains several useful reproductions but its treatment of the symbolism is to me unpersuasive. The same scholar discusses briefly the Castle of Love motif in *Ivory* (New York: Putnam, 1965), 47–48.

Figs. 2a and b. *Siege of the Castle of Love.* Double illumination from Walter de Milemete, *De nobilitatibus, sapientiis, et prudentiis regum.* 1326–27. Christ Church, Oxford. Photo courtesy of The Beinecke Rare Book and Manuscript Library, Yale University.

Figs. 2a and b. *Siege of the Castle of Love.* Double illumination from Walter de Milemete, *De nobilitatibus, sapientiis, et prudentiis regum.* 1326–27. Christ Church, Oxford. Photo courtesy of The Beinecke Rare Book and Manuscript Library, Yale University.

Fig. 3. *Siege of the Castle of Love*. Ivory casket. Fourteenth century. Victoria and Albert Museum, London.

be an implication that the conquest of this kind of castle begins with displays of macho prowess.

In several ivories, like one presently in Cracow (Fig. 4), some of the women in the inner panels above are clearly watching the tournament outside the walls. Here both assault and resistance are limited to the right-hand panel, and even there on the topmost level we find a couple embracing next to defenders tossing their roses. The upper middle panels mingle spectators with another couple, and to the left an erotic conquest is carried to the point of abduction. The topmost vignette shows an affectionate couple flanked by a musician and a servant with roses and garland; below, the knight rides away with his mistress on his horse. The final scene of the elopement at the lower left shows the couple embracing in a skiff piloted by a boatman. In ivories like this one, comedy seems to have given way to romance, as the ferocity of the defense has yielded to tenderness. But it must be admitted that these images as a set are not easy to interpret; they open up a hermeneutic space where various components of male compulsion, pressure, display, seductiveness, and gentleness are mingled with degrees of female resistance and surrender. It isn't even clear which gender is in control, if either. One could write a scenario following a male fantasy by which vigorous effort and aggression conquer inferior powers of resistance. But in view of the female patronage for these objects, one might hypothesize a converse female fantasy, whereby the knights are allured by feminine charm to display their skill in jousting and expend their energies in climbing walls before falling to their knees in symbolic surrender. The god of love, in his frequent appearances on these ivories, always stations himself on the battlements with the women defenders; his presence might be taken to imply that in the mythical world of these images, women exercise the real erotic control. If medieval women largely led a life of enclosure, here arguably is a Utopian female enclosure which men want to enter but can only do so as courtly

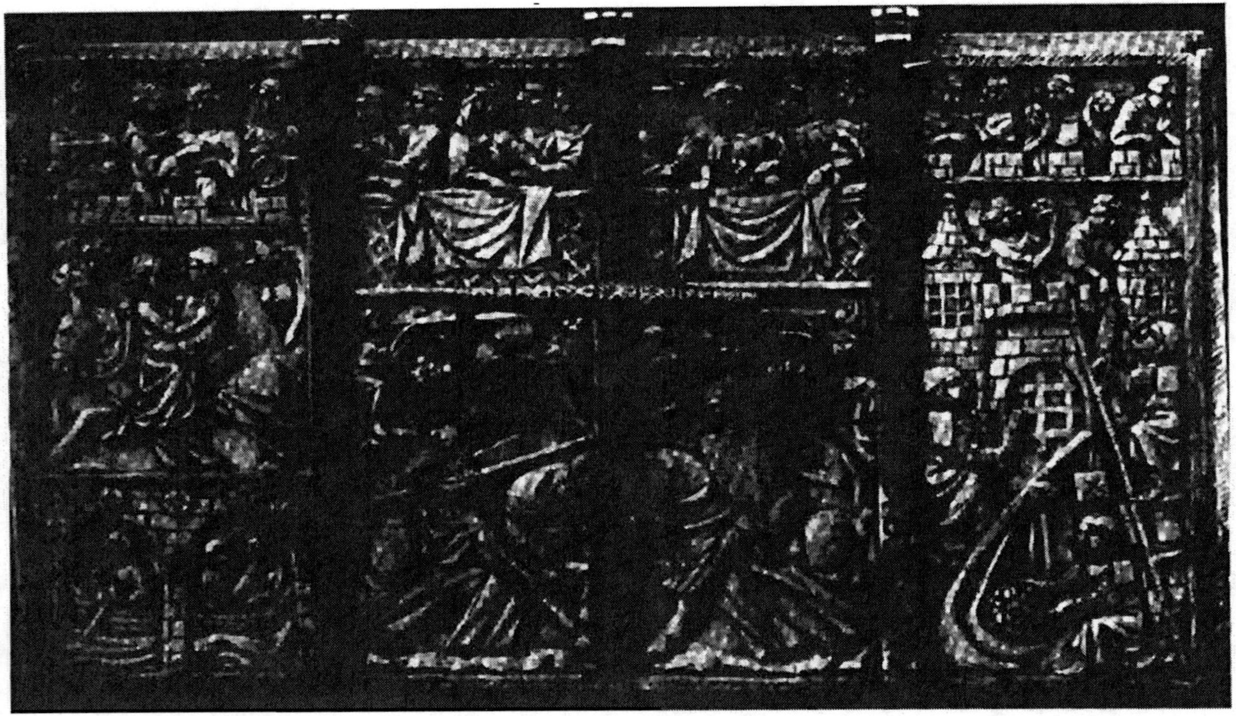

Fig. 4. *Siege of the Castle of Love*. Ivory casket. Fourteenth century. Treasury of the Cracow cathedral.

servants, and which women finally leave on terms of intimate equality.

However they are interpreted, we have records of many other lost objects in inventories which represented similar dramatic situations. We hear for example of a fountain made in 1364–65 for Louis of Anjou which represented a castle whose battlements are defended by ladies with maces and shields. We hear of an arras made in 1397 and belonging to the duke of Gloucester depicting an assault on ladies in a castle.[10] We also have tantalizing records of continental courtly festivities involving a castle of love which may well have acted out a siege.[11] It is unlikely that William Cornish first invented this device for court entertainment. Our history of this motif is almost certainly incomplete. One way to fill it out would be to bring in the numerous analogues, both religious and profane, which locate themselves slightly outside the precise motif but resemble this kind of siege more or less closely. To list all those analogues would require more than a single lecture and doubtless more than one scholar's knowledge. But among them, one would have to mention Robert Grosseteste's *Chateau d'amour*, Christine de Pisan's *Cité des dames*, the English morality play *The Castle of*

[10] This and other citations from inventories are given by Loomis, "Allegorical Siege," 260–61. See also Koechlin, 1: 403–4.

[11] An intriguing example can be found in A. Rosie, " 'Morisques' and 'Momeryes': Aspects of Court Entertainment at the Court of Savoy in the Fifteenth Century," in *Power, Culture, and Religion in France, c. 1350–c.1550*, ed. Christopher Allmand (Woodbridge, Suffolk: Boydell Press, 1989), 67. On the general theme, see Sidney Anglo, "The Evolution of the Early Tudor Disguising, Pageant, and Mask," *Renaissance Drama* , n.s. 1 (1968): 3–44, and *Spectacle, Pageantry, and Early Tudor Policy* (Oxford: Clarendon, 1969), chapter 3. See also George R. Kernodle, *From Art to Theatre* (Chicago: Univ. of Chicago Press, 1944), 76–84, and Kernodle's article with Portia Kernodle, "Dramatic Aspects of the Medieval Tournament," *Speech Monographs* 9 (1942): 161–72, esp. 170–71.

*Perseveraunce* (where female virtues within the castle successfully repel the assault of male vices with a fusillade of roses),[12] a poem by the Grand Rhetoriqueur Jean Molinet entitled "Le Hault Siege d'Amours,"[13] the castle of the sorceress Dragontina in Boiardo's *Orlando Innamorato* (1.9.66ff.), and the intimidating city of women in Ariosto's *Orlando Furioso* (19.54–20.95). Christine's work suggests the need of women for their own protective community, and Ariosto's somewhat nasty episode suggests male fears of such a community. Above all, in listing analogues to the castle of ladies, one would need to recall the fortress of Jealousy defended by the giant Danger in the *Roman de la Rose*, a fortress built to protect the rose from the lover and

---

[12] Pride, Wrath, and Envy, led by Belial, speak of their attack on Charity, Patience, and Meekness in distinctly gendered terms. Belial rallies his cohorts:

> Have don, ye boyes, al at onys!
> Lasche don these moderys, all three! . . .
> Have do, boyes blo and blake!
> Wirke these wenchys wo and wrake!

But the rain of roses from the castle routs the attackers. Wrath emerges battered from the fray:

> I am al betyn blak and blo
> With a rose that on rode was rent.
> My speche is almost spent.
> Hir [Patience's] rosys fel on me so scharpe
> That mine hed hangith as an harpe.

"The Castle of Perseverance," lines 2188–89. 2195–96, 2219–23, in *Medieval Drama*, ed. David M. Bevington (Boston: Houghton Mifflin, 1975), 860–61.

[13] Molinet's somewhat incoherent poem of 400 lines consists largely of a dialogue between the despairing "Amant" and the comforting "Espoir," but it concludes with an attack inspired by the *Roman de la Rose* on the tower of love defended by the god "Amours," who calls upon the "demoiselles" who share the fortress with him to assist in its defense. The poem ends without a resolution. See *Les Faictz et dictz de Jean Molinet*, ed. Noel Dupire, vol. 2 (Paris: Société des anciens textes français, 1937), 569–83.

to imprison Bel Accueil (Fair Welcoming).[14] That castle resists an attack by the lover and his allies in the second part of the poem, but it is finally reduced when Venus sets it afire, thus allowing the lover to gather the rose and the poem to end.[15] Clearly this castle would have been widely influential, but we need to remember that the Treviso *ludus* had already been performed in 1214 when the *Roman* was written. Jean de Meun didn't invent the assault on that kind of castle.

One might ask about all this body of heterogeneous material—legendary, folkloric, poetic, decorative, festive, courtly, from at least four centuries and at least four countries—one might ask whether there is anything *represented* by the siege of the castle of ladies, anything signified which calls for interpretation, or whether the materials are too scattered and too insubstantial to support the weight of hermeneutic analysis. My own inclination is to say yes, a very great deal is represented and indeed so much that it can't be reduced to a single formula. Thus far we have clearly seen a struggle between the genders for sexual control, always initiated by male aggression. Some of the implications of that assault are very troubling, since the use of male violence, even symbolic violence, to subdue female resistance must always invite a potentially ugly reading. However funny or romantic or festive this image appears, the sombre shadow of rape darkens its range of appropriate interpretations, a shadow already explicit in Cosmas of Prague. But I would argue that there *is* a range of interpretive options as the motif develops, options depending on

---

[14] The story of this fortress (*forterece, tor, chastel*) begins at line 3605 of the text of the *Roman de la Rose* edited by Félix Lecoy (Paris: Champion, 1965), 1:111. For an English version, see *The Romance of the Rose* by Guillaume de Lorris and Jean de Meun, trans. Charles Dahlberg (Princeton: Princeton Univ. Press, 1971), 82ff.

[15] The attack begins at line 15,103 of part 2; Venus throws her burning brand into the castle at line 21,221. See *The Romance of the Rose*, 257 and 347.

the given representation. As we have seen, the outcomes of the conflict vary, as do the assumptions concerning the conflict. One might say that the fantasies differ. Once one begins to interpret a motif like this one, the temptation arises to look for a central signification which would explain each instance, but for the moment I want to resist that temptation. Given the continuity of the motif, its occasions, its cultures, its audiences, its media were so various that a precise and rigid interpretation is unlikely to fit all the cases. We will even meet with some assaults where the principal conflict is not in fact between men and women. The allegorical siege would seem to be so open a sign that any given instance has to be considered in its own terms.

That consideration might lead us back to our most fully documented dramatization, the disguising for Arthur and Catherine in 1501. The particular circumstances of that staging were epithalamic, and any interpretation of its symbolism ought to begin with this context. It is worth noting that the epithalamic convention of the Renaissance, derived in turn from poetic conventions of antiquity, represented the bride as fearful of the ordeal she supposed to be awaiting her. The ancient Roman poem which established the convention was Catullus's no. 61, where "tardet ingenuus pudor" ("noble shame delays") the bride on her way to the bedchamber, and where she weeps at the necessity to enter it, "flet, quod ire necesse est."[16] That conventional reluctance was attributed to the bride by Renaissance epithalamists like Marot, Jonson, and Herrick. "Shrinke not, soft Virgin," wrote Ben Jonson, "you will love / Anon what you so feare to prove." "Tu n'en doibs faire pleurs," wrote Marot, addressing the royal princess Renée de France, and in another "Chant nuptial" for another princess, he resurrected a figure we know from the *Roman de la rose*: "Danger fier, & rebelle/ N'y a

[16] Catullus, no. 61, lines 79, 81.

que voir" (Proud and headstrong Danger has no place here).[17] We have no sure way of knowing how often the convention corresponded to lived experience, but it is unlikely that no such fears existed in a society of arranged marriages. In any case, the formal presumption was that brides did shrink from their defloration as Spenser's Amoret did, so that every wedding night did supposedly witness a sexual forcing which was nonetheless necessary to society and which eventually would give the young wife pleasure.

That convention would offer a plausible way to understand Cornish's disguising. There is of course much that we can't know about it; much would depend on the *tone* of the performance, on the relative high spirits or the dramatic realism of the assault on the castle. The account we have would suggest that the tone was not cordial. When the envoys Hope and Desire request the favors of the ladies for the knights they represent, the answer seems to have been sharp:

---

[17] *Ben Jonson*, ed. C. H. Herford and P. and E. Simpson, 11 vols. (Oxford: Clarendon Press, 1925–52), 7:225. Clément Marot, *Oeuvres poétiques*, ed. Gérard Defaux (Paris: Classiques Garnier, 1990), 350 and 362. Among the many other instances of this topos, one can cite a stanza from Robert Herrick's "Epithalamie to Sir Thomas Southwell and his Ladie":

> Is it (sweet maid) your fault these holy
> Bridall-Rites goe on so slowly?
>   Deare, is it this you dread,
>   The losse of Maiden-head?
>   Beleeve me; you will most
>   Esteeme it when 'tis lost:
>   Then it no longer keep,
>   Lest Issue lye asleep.

*The Poetical Works of Robert Herrick*, ed. L. C. Martin (Oxford: Clarendon Press, 1963), 53.

An earlier essay of mine discussed briefly the 1501 disguising and quoted the lines from Jonson: "Magic and Festivity at the Renaissance Court," *Renaissance Quarterly* 40 (1987): 641–44.

> The seid ladies gave their finall aunswere of uttirly refuse and knowladge of any such company, or that they were ever myndid to thaccomplisshement of any such requestes, and pleynly denyed ther purpos and desire.

The envoys, for their part, seeing their embassy thwarted, resort to open threats.

> The two seid ambassadoures, therwith takyng great displeasure, shewed the seid ladies that the knightes wolde for this unkyend refusell make bataill and assault, so and in such wise, them and ther castell, that it shuld be grevous to abyde there power and malesse.

"Malesse" here does not have its modern meaning but evoked something closer to our word "aggressiveness." Aggressive at any rate the knights proved to be, as the account goes on to declare.

> [The knights], therwith not beyng content, with moch males and curragyous myend, alitide from the seid mount with their baners displayed and hastely spede theim to the rehercyd castell, which they forthwith assaultid so and in such wise that the ladies, yeldyng themselvys, descendid from the seid castell and submittid them to the pouer, grace, and will of thoes noble knightes.

If this is to be read in terms of the epithalamic context, the ladies' resistance corresponds to the fears of the bride faced with the husband's conjugal violence. In that light, the resistance is perceived as understandable but anti-social, so that the sharpness of the denial justifies the vigor of the assault. My attempt here is not to justify what happened that night but to understand without anachronism the mentality of a remote society. The woman according to this construal would be released from the claustration of her resistance to conjugal and social integration, and her yielding of the castle would correspond to her refusal further to shrink from the roles society requires of her.

> Thoes noble knightes beyng right freshly disguysid, and the ladies also, iiijor of them aftir thenglissh fachyon, and thothir iiijor aftir the maner of Hispayne, dauncyd toguyders dyvers and many goodly daunces.

The leading forth of the eight ladies to dance would symbolize a process of civilization which was also a union of two nations, represented equally on the dance floor by two styles of dress. Sir Thomas Elyot would write in *The Boke Named the Governour* that "by the association of a man and a woman in daunsinge may be signified matrimonie."[18] Here the agreement to dance symbolizes the reconciliation of women to their participation in the dance of society, a participation at once emotional, sexual, and communal. We can recognize that symbolism of the dance, but we are also obliged to recognize the symbolic implications of the assault, which estheticizes the sexual forcing of the conjugal bed. The aggressiveness of the assault on this occasion, the "malés," does not bespeak compassion for female hesitation.

It is notable that Catherine, who is impersonated in the disguising, is not represented among the reluctant inmates of the castle. The goodly and fair lady "in her apparell like unto the Princes of Hispayne" rides on the second pageant car, the ship. She is physically and allegorically separated from that resistance she might have been expected to be feeling or to have felt. This separation could be interpreted as a gesture of tact: *this* bride could not be acknowledged to feel what weaker brides feel. *She* is above the shrinking of lesser women. Or else the separation could be construed as a lesson to Catherine: how *could* she resist the embraces of an English prince? At any rate, the Catherine figure in the disguising is the only participant with nothing to

[18] Sir Thomas Elyot, *The Boke Named the Governour*, ed. H. H. S. Croft (New York: Burt Franklin, 1967), 1:233.

do. It is woman in general, Spanish woman and English woman, who is led from the castle and engaged in a dance where the national costumes are equally distributed.

The wisdom of respecting the specificity of the occasion before reaching interpretive conclusions is illustrated by the two Tudor court entertainments which repeated the siege and which presented King Henry VIII performing as an assailant of a castle of ladies. Both of these recall superficially the disguising for Catherine, but the resemblances are misleading. On New Year's night of 1512, according to Edward Hall's *Chronicles*, six ladies defended "le Fortresse dangerus" against six knights led by the king, but in this case the resistance appears to have been minimal.

> The ladies seyng [the attackers] so lustie and coragious, wer content to solace with them, and upon farther communicacion, to yeld the castle, and so thei came doune and daunced a long space. And after the ladies led the knightes into the castle, and then the castle sodainly vanished, out of their sightes.

This sounds much more like a male fantasy of seduction requiring little if any force, although the fascinating name of the fortress may complicate slightly the task of interpretation. It is perhaps significant that Catherine, now queen, was not a participant opposite her husband in this masquerade, although she was present, as she was at the assault in 1522, sponsored by Cardinal Wolsey, upon the *Schatew vert*. On that occasion the women inside the castle were given names such as "Beautie," "Kindnes," "Bountie," and "Pitie." The group of assailants included the king; among their number were figures named "Youth," "Loyaltie," "Pleasure," and "Libertie." Spokesman for the attackers was a certain "Ardent Desire," probably played by Cornish. What was new at the Schatew Vert was a group of supposedly female defenders outside the walls, in fact boys dressed as Indian women, named "Dangier," "Disdain," "Gelousie," "Unkyndenes," "Scorn," "Malebouche," and "Straungenes." The ladies inside the walls were content to yield the place, but, writes Hall,

> Scorne and Disdain saied they would holde the place, then Desire saied the ladies should be wonne ... then the lordes ranne to the castle ... and the ladies defended the castle with Rose water and Comfittes, and the lordes threwe in Dates and Orenges ... but at the last the place was wonne, but Lady Scorne and her compaignie stubbernely defended them with boows and balles, till they were driven out of the place and fled.

The disappearance of these blocking figures permits the ritual conclusion of the dance.[19]

The particular aggressiveness of Lady Scorn and her company is underscored by their weapons: they used bows and balls, although we can only guess what they actually did with them. But the lords used dates and oranges and the ladies rosewater and comfits, these latter being a kind of candied fruit. We can note parenthetically the curious continuity in the missiles employed in these assaults from our first example at Treviso. There the missiles already included fruit, flowers, and rosewater. Now, three hundred years later, they are still the weapons of choice. (I think we can assume that these were also the missiles at the 1501 disguising, although our report fails to describe them.) The manuscript illustrations and ivories douse everyone with roses. How exactly does one interpret these non-weapons? We seem

[19] The 1512 and 1522 disguisings are described by Edward Hall in his *Chronicle containing the History of England* (London: Cadell and Davies, 1809), 526 and 631 respectively. Sidney Anglo supplements Hall's accounts with archival research in his "The Evolution of the Early Tudor Mask" (see n. 11 above). For the "Schatew Vert," see also E. W. Ives, *Anne Boleyn* (Oxford: Blackwell, 1986), 47–49.

to find an estheticization of sexual conflict in which nobody gets hurt. One discerns a male fantasy that the pursuit of a woman will never encounter anything more dangerous than flowers. And in the elopements on some of the ivories, images designed for female consumers, one may also discern a fantasy that the rose-tinted struggle leads to the true love of an intrepid suitor. But this kind of benign interpretation can also be reversed. The images of siege and struggle might be read conversely as underscoring the real conflict which is partly screened by social decorum. Considered this way, the flowers and fruit tend to suggest the sweetened words and conventions which half-conceal the true sexual struggle depicted.

Having noted this, we need now to observe that the Schatew Vert disguising, with its three-sided conflict, really opens up new hermeneutic possibilities. What had earlier appeared to be a struggle between men and women is metamorphosed here into a three-way struggle between male desire, female responsiveness, and female resistance. Three banners hung before the castle bore emblems implying female erotic dominion; on one, three hearts torn apart; on the second "a ladies hand gripyng a mans harte"; on the third "a ladies hand turnyng a mannes hart [upside down]." These emblematic declarations of female dominance anticipate the action, where the conflict between the genders is apparently subordinated to a symbolic conflict within a female mind. Dangier, the leader of the defenders, we have already met as the giant who protected the rose in the *Roman de la Rose*; in one recent translation, he is called simply "Resistance."[20] Dangier, in fact, like Gelousie and Malebouche, is a survivor from the famous *Roman*, as are the compassionate ladies Beautie, Kindnes, and Pitie.[21] What emerges from this staging is a po-

[20] Dahlberg, *Romance of the Rose, passim.*

[21] According to the OED (Definition 2.a), the noun "danger" in 1522

tential conflict within a female psyche confronted with desire, like that memorable conflict evoked by Guillaume de Lorris and Jean de Meun. The crucial figure is now neither wholly masculine nor wholly feminine; it is the tertiary figure Dangier who stands for one suspicious, prudent voice in the feminine mind. If, in looking at our fourteenth-century ivories, we were puzzled by an apparent inconsistency in the conduct of the female defenders, that inconsistency may have been part of the point. In retrospect, the name of the "Fortresse dangerus" in the disguising of 1512 now seems to contain a pun. That fortress had been "garnished with artilerie, and weapon after the moste warlike fashion," but it had not really been very perilous for its attackers. The true "danger" may have been the signified which the fortress symbolized, female resistance to male seduction or force. This interpretation would displace the symbolic struggle, or complicate it, away from the conflict of genders for erotic control towards a conflict within a woman's mind for control of her conduct, that inner conflict which is the implicit action of the *Roman de la Rose.*

The centrality of Danger, and thus of internal female conflict, in the castle of ladies at the opening of the sixteenth century is confirmed by a tapestry woven at that time in Flanders which conveniently labels its figures with abstract names (Fig. 5). Here the assailants do not represent anything like male aggression, but simply the forces of Danger and his male allies, among them Malebouche, Vilonie, and Faultedesens. On the battlements of the castle appear the ladies Plaisance, Leaulté, Largesse, and Espoer, who are armed with roses and are clearly repelling the attackers. Above them, "Obedience" and "Dignité" are crowning

---

could still mean "difficulty (made or raised); hesitation, reluctance, chariness, stint, grudging, coyness." The first usage in this sense is dated 1290 and the last 1526.

Fig. 5. *Siege of the Castle of Love.* Flemish tapestry, probably woven in Brussels. Early sixteenth century.

"Secret des Dames," seated on a throne. There are still other figures in this crowded image, but there is no Ardent Desire, no male principle at all. The only conflict in sight is the conflict within the female mind between Danger and Largesse, between resistance and generosity. The fortress is no longer *guarded* by Danger but assaulted by him unsuccessfully, and the designer has clearly striven to render him and his cohorts thoroughly unattractive.[22]

We meet the same antagonist in the episode of Spenser's *Faerie Queene* which stems most directly from the tradition of the allegorical siege. When in book four of that poem the lover Scudamour wants to penetrate the Temple of Venus to abduct the virginal Amoret, he finds that he must first enter the castle surrounding that temple, a castle defended by a giant whose name is Daunger. This guardian, Scudamour reports, "full many did affray, that else faine enter would."(IV.x.16)[23] So grim was Daunger's face, says Scudamour, that many who wished to pass through the gate were deterred by the sternness of his look, but for these the young lover has only contempt:

> Unworthy they of grace, whom one deniall
> Excludes from fairest hope, withouten further triall.
> (IV.x.17)

---

[22] This tapestry is described by Loomis in "Allegorical Siege," 261–63, and is reproduced as Plate IV in his article. Loomis found it in Jules Guiffrey's *Histoire Générale de la Tapisserie*, vol. 3. But the closest description of the tapestry is to be found in the catalogue of the "Musée Retrospectif" of 1876 sponsored by the Union Centrale des Beaux-Arts in Paris. This tapestry, "le siège du chateau d'amour," is numbered 269 in that catalogue. I owe this information and a copy of the description to the kindness of Mr. Robert Wenley of the Wallace Collection in London. The tapestry was owned by Sir Richard Wallace in 1876, but, according to Mr. Wenley, was later sold and has disappeared from view.

[23] Quotations from Spenser are taken from Edmund Spenser, *The Faerie Queene*, ed. A. C. Hamilton (London: Longman, 1984).

This seems to mean that a suitor should never be deterred by initial discouragement. Spenser's figure of Daunger actually raises a problem which is familiar in the later twentieth century, the problem of interpreting sexual signals, and Spenser doesn't seem to take the position we would want him to. Scudamour at any rate easily disposes of this paper monster, and ultimately makes his way to the penetralia of the temple, where, with the encouragement of Venus, he manfully leads Amoret away, disregarding the protests of Womanhood and resolutely ignoring the pleas of the lady herself.

> She often prayd, and often me besought,
> Sometime with tender teares to let her goe,
> Sometime with witching smyles; but yet for nought,
> That ever she to me could say or doe,
> Could she her wished freedome fro me wooe;
> But forth I led her through the Temple gate. . . .
>
> (IV.x.57)

Scudamour here sounds like a caricature of fatuous egotism, and his much-heralded conquest begins to look again like ritualized violence. But as all Spenserians know, nothing in this poem is ever as simple as it first appears, and the reader is obliged to remember that this same Amoret runs to her lover in ecstatic union after their separation by the enchanter Busirane:

> . . . she faire Lady overcommen quight
> Of huge affection, did in pleasure melt,
> And in sweete ravishment pourd out her spright.
>
> (III.xii.45, 1590 edition)

This is the most intense moment of sexual pleasure *The Faerie Queene* ever reaches, too intense perhaps to be preserved in the poem. Can it be reconciled with Amoret's protests during her abduction on the way to the wedding altar? One vulgar way to formulate a reconciliation would be to attribute to Spenser the notion that beneath Amoret's protests, she really wanted to be abducted. But Spenser is seldom so crude as that. A reading more faithful to his text, more faithful to the *Roman de la Rose* and to the motif of the allegorical siege, would suggest that sexuality is genuinely confusing, and not least to the uninitiated. A sexual decision *can* divide the mind; it can allure and terrify at once; it can on occasion produce truly mixed signals, although these must never be misused as alibis for violence. The figure of Danger, and the psychic phenomenon that corresponds to that figure as it was handed down through the centuries, seem to bespeak an understandable hesitation by women before erotic temptation.

I pointed out above that the assault on the castle of ladies carries with it as one interpretive option the implication of rape. But as I understand the giant Danger, his presence precludes that option. Danger is an embodiment of female reluctance in the code of courtly love, and thus a figure whose presence guarantees some degree of female control. Danger is a powerful giant when the reluctance matters, when it may well be determinant. Danger doesn't live in the same world as Christine de Pisan when she writes: "I am ... troubled and grieved when men argue that many women want to be raped and that it does not bother them at all to be raped by men even when they verbally protest."[24] Christine there is dealing with horror, with a situation without ambiguity. But in the realm of experience on this side of that extremity, ambiguities abound because ambivalences

[24] Christine de Pizan, *The Book of the City of Ladies*, tr. E. J. Richards (New York: Persea Books, 1988), 160–61. "Si m'anuye et m'esgriesve de ce que hommes dient tant que femmes se veullent efforcier et qu'il ne leur desplait mie, quoyque elles escondissent de bouche, d'estre par hommes efforciees." Maureen Cheney Curnow, "The 'Livre de la cité des dames' of Christine de Pisan: a critical edition" (Ph.D. diss., Vanderbilt University, 1975), 2:885.

abound, and possibly these ambivalences nourish the dramatic interest of the castle of ladies which resists and yields. Ambivalences may well exist before the prospect of a wedding as before the prospect of a sexual involvement. The risk for the suitor of negotiating those ambivalences is already dramatized in the *Roman de la Rose*, when the lover is scolded for overinterpreting the favorable disposition of Bel Accueil (Fair Welcoming). "You understood poorly what Fair Welcoming offered you when he allowed you to speak to him," the lover is told. "He gladly offered you his goods, but only in an honest way."[25] That capacity for misunderstanding what is often hard to understand seems to be inscribed in western sexuality, and of course it is sometimes compounded by the wish to misunderstand.

The collective imagination which produced the allegorical siege seems to have recognized intermittently that figure who is being crowned above the tumult in the Flemish tapestry, the "Secret des Dames," the secrecy of ladies, which I take to represent the right of women to deliberate privately over romantic decisions. The playful rituals at Treviso and Fribourg sẹem to have acted out as a game the perennial tensions not only between men and women but also between prudence and temptation, and if temptation won most frequently, the victory still remained within the boundaries of the *ludus*. It is true that the brawl which the game produced in 1214 illustrates the fragility of those boundaries. Instabilities of conduct underlie instabilities of meaning.

---

[25] *Romance of the Rose*, 253.

Malement antandre savez
ce que Bel Acueil vos offri
quant parler a lui vos soffri.
Ses biens vos offroit lieement,
mes que ce fust honestement.

*Roman de la Rose*, lines 14818–22.

One might conclude that the space opened up by the attack on the castle of ladies is both the space of negotiations between the genders—rhetorical, violent, or intimate—*and* the space for negotiations within an individual mind, where the intrigue can be even more insidious and confusing. The God of Love on those ivory caskets stands side by side with women on the battlements and aims his arrows at the attackers. But if the arrows of Eros find their mark, presumably the assault can only grow more heated. Is the god of love at odds with the women who are his ostensible allies? Perhaps the duality of his position coincides with the duality of theirs. But women of course have no monopoly on duality; those who might be tempted to think so need only remember the standoff in the Oxford manuscript, where the gestures of the harassed knights betray their strategic bewilderment. Perhaps the difficulty of understanding the ivories and the illuminations—the difficulty really of understanding the siege of the castle of ladies in all its forms—corresponds to the difficulty of understanding erotic politics.

By the seventeenth century, the energies of this siege would be refined and dissipated across the allegorical map of the Carte de Tendre, Mlle. de Scudéry's decorous and precious redrawing of the lines of erotic negotiations. On that imaginary landscape, men have to make their way patiently from town to town before reaching their goal, the unfortified city of Tendre, but their odyssey is threatened by the hazards of disastrous itineraries. The Carte de Tendre in its own way underscores the subtle hazards of tender feelings, and one of its more prominent obstacles is a certain Mer Dangereuse. In that landscape, erotic ambiguities are alive and well.[26]

---

[26] [Madeleine] de Scudéry, *Clélie, Histoire romaine* (Paris: Louys Billaine, 1666), 1:399–405. The text does not authorize a double meaning of "dangereuse" alluding to the *Roman de la rose*, but it does evoke the possibility of conflicting affective impulses in women's minds. The "Mer Dangereuse" is

But there had been one more allegorical siege during the sixteenth century which was calculated to suppress any potential ambiguities. This was the charade staged in 1581 by four gentlemen of the Elizabethan court, including Sir Philip Sidney and Fulke Greville, at a time when Queen Elizabeth appeared favorably disposed to the courtship of the Duc d'Alençon. Sidney and his friends, deeply opposed to this marriage, found a way to dramatize the queen's *in*accessibility in front of an audience of French ambassadors by failing to capture "The Fortresse of Perfect Beautie" in which Elizabeth was placed. After two days of tilting, the Foster Children of Desire, as they called themselves, acknowledged their failure to capture the fortress and thereby dramatized the queen's impervious isolation from *all* suitors.[27] The message of this performance to the French ambassadors was the uselessness of a siege. Here for once a woman was assigned total control; here there was no negotiation and no surrender.

To return once again to the disguising of 1501, our report on that evening contains an epilogue which with the hindsight of history is rich in ironies. It can serve as an epilogue for this paper. When the disguising was over on November 19th, the bridegroom, Prince Arthur, made a brief appearance on the dance floor, but not with his bride. He executed two bass dances with a certain Lady Cecil; later the Princess Catherine danced with one of her Spanish ladies-in-waiting. Nobody, it seems, was throwing the sixteen-year-old bride into the arms of her fifteen-year-old husband, in spite of the ritual bedding on the night of

so-called "parce qu'il est assez dangereux à une Femme, d'aller un peu au delà des dernieres Bornes de l'amitié; & elle [Clélie, the cartographer] fait en suite qu'au delà de cette Mer, c'est ce que nous appellons *Terres inconnuës*, parce qu'en effet nous ne scavons point ce qu'il y a" (405).

[27] "The Four Foster Children of Desire" in *Entertainments for Elizabeth I*, ed. Jean Wilson (Totowa, N.J.: Rowman and Littlefield, 1980), 63–85.

their marriage. But the end of the Friday evening after the disguising belonged to the future king, the ten-year-old Henry, duke of York, who erupted on the scene with that animal energy England would later come to know well.

> Thirde and last cam doun the Duke of York, havyng with him the Lady Margaret his sister on his hond, and dauncyd two baas daunces. And aftirward he, perceyvyng himself to be accombred with his clothis, sodenly cast of his gowne, and dauncyd in his jaket with the seid Lady Margaret in so goodly and pleasaunt maner that hit was to the Kyng and Quene right great and singler pleasure.

Catherine of Aragon could not have guessed that night what this ebullient appearance augured for her future. But as we know, the boy Arthur Tudor would die within five months. Eight years later, Henry would be king of England and Catherine his queen. Many years after that, Henry would worry, or pretend to worry, that he had committed incest with his brother Arthur's wife. That anxiety, real or imaginary, would not only lead to a divorce with Catherine but to the English reformation. Catherine however maintained that what was regarded as incest had not occurred, and on June 21, 1529, she confronted her husband publicly at Blackfriars before a solemn assembly which included two cardinals. At the most dramatic moment of her personal defense, she touched upon the most delicate and crucial question. Speaking directly to her husband in that formal gathering, she said:

> When ye had me at the first, I take God to be my judge, I was a true maid, without touch of man. And whether this be true or no, I put it to your conscience.

She paused for an answer, but no answer was forthcoming.[28] She would lose her battle, and the reformation of the English church would proceed. But that momentous process depended on a doubtful presumption that in 1501 Arthur's hope and desire had been effective, and that he had in fact succeeded in capturing Catherine's castle.[29]

---

[28] Garrett Mattingly, *Catherine of Aragon* (Boston: Little, Brown and Company, 1941), 286.

[29] I would like to thank Ms. Jennifer Morrison for her tireless and resourceful assistance in the preparation of this essay.

# *Appendix:*

# *Extract from* Cosmas of Prague*

Quia ea tempestate virgines huius terre sine iugo pubescentes veluti Amazones militaria arma affectantes et sibi ductrices facientes pari modo uti tirones militabant, venacionibus per silvas viriliter insistebant, non eas viri, sed ipsemet sibi viros, quos et quando voluerunt, accipiebant, et . . . vir et femina in habitu nullum discrimen habebant. Unde in tantum feminea excrevit audacia, ut in quadam rupe non longe a predicta urbe [Prague] oppidum natura loci firmum sibi construerent, cui a virginali vocabulo inditum est nomen Devin. Quod videntes iuvenes contra eas nimio zelo indignantes multo plures insimul conglobati non longius quam unius bucine in altera rupe inter arbusta edificant urbem, quam moderni nuncupant Wissegrad, tunc autem ab arbustis taxerat nomen Hvrasten. Et quia sepe virgines sollertiores ad decipiendos iuvenes fiebant, sepe autem iuvenes virginibus fortiores existebant, modo bellum, modo pax inter eos agebatur. Et dum interposita pace pociuntur, placuit utrisque partibus, ut componerent cibis et potibus symbolum et per tres dies sine armis sollempnem insimul agerent ludum in constituto loco. Quid plura? Non aliter iuvenes cum puellis ineunt convivia, ac si lupi rapaces querentes edulia, ut intrarent ovilia. Primam diem epulis et nimiis potibus hilarem ducunt.

> Dumque volunt sedare sitim, sitis altera crevit.
> Leticiamque suam iuvenes vix noctis ad horam differunt.
> Nox erat et celo fulgebat luna sereno,
> Inflans tunc lituum dedit unus eis ita signum dicens:
> "Lusistis satis, edistis satis atque bibistis;
> Surgite, vos rauco clamat Venus aurea sistro."

Moxque singuli singulas rapuere puellas. Mane autem facto iam pacis inito pacto, sublatis Cerere et Bacho ex earum oppido muros Lemniaco vacuos indulgent Vulcano. Et ex illa tempestate post obitum principis Lubosse sunt mulieres nostrates virorum sub potestate.

[Because at that time the unbridled pubescent girls of the region set out to bear arms like Amazons and assumed the rank of officers as well as of recruits in battle, pursuing game through the forests like men, they received whatever men at whatever time they wished, rather than the contrary, and . . . men and women observed no distinction in their dress. Whereupon female boldness grew to such a degree that they built themselves a town on a certain cliff not far from the aforesaid city [Prague], a town easy to defend from the nature of the site, to which the name of "Devin" ["Castle of the Maidens"] was given from the word for "maiden." When the young men saw this, excessively offended as they were by the girls, they banded together in much larger numbers to build another city on a woody cliff, no further from the first than the distance of a bugle call, which today is called

"Wissegrad" but then took the name "Hvrasten" from the surrounding woods. And because the maidens often showed themselves more apt at snatching the youths, but often the youths considered themselves to be stronger, they alternated between war and peace. And once while a truce was agreed to, it pleased both sides to organize a common meal with food and drink and to hold formal festivities without weapons for three days in an appointed place. What more is there to say? The young men entered upon the banqueting with the girls like greedy wolves entering a sheepfold in search of food. On the first day their spirits rise from the food and excessive drink. While the men try to satisfy their thirst, another kind of thirst arises, and they can scarcely wait for their pleasure at nightfall. Then it was night, and as the moon shone from a tranquil sky, one of them blew a horn as a signal and alerted the others by calling: "You have sported enough; you have eaten and drunk enough; arise! beautiful Venus calls you with her harsh rattle." And soon each man seized his girl. In the morning, having entered upon a peace treaty and carried grain and wine out from the girls' town, they offered its empty walls to Lemnian Vulcan. And since that time, after the death of queen Lubosse, our wives have always remained under the authority of their husbands.]

*Taken from *Cosmae Pragensis Chronica Boemorum*, vol. 2 of *Monumenta Germaniae Historica* (Berlin: Weidmann, 1923) 19–21. My translation. The lines printed as verse echo more or less closely passages in Ovid (*Metamorphoses* 3.415), Horace (*Epodes* 15.1; *Epistulae* 2.2.214), and Virgil (*Aeneid*, 8.696). I owe this reference to my colleague Peter Demetz.

# *The Aldo S. Bernardo Fund*

The Aldo S. Bernardo Fund is the endowment fund for the Center for Medieval and Early Renaissance Studies at the State University of New York at Binghamton. Established in 1989 by a gift from the founding co-director of the Center, the Fund aims to support Center programs with a special emphasis on Medieval and Renaissance Italian studies. The governing body of the Fund, working with the Executive Council of the Center, has determined that the Bernardo Fund will first support a lecture program and book purchases for the Bartle Library. As the endowment develops, it will support the broad range of programs associated with the Center's teaching and research activities.

The Foundation of the State University of New York at Binghamton, which is a private, not-for-profit corporation chartered under the laws of the State of New York, receives tax-deductible donations on behalf of the Bernardo Fund.